FROM MANET
to WARHOL

Written and illustrated by David Armitage

CollinsEducational

An Imprint of HarperCollinsPublishers

Contents

Introduction

The paintings of the 19th century Impressionists are available nowadays as prints, posters, postcards, on mugs, T-shirts and even umbrellas. They are enjoyed by people all over the world.

The Impressionists had a major effect on the way that artists worked during the 20th century and it is possible to follow their **influences** through the years. The styles that developed, the use of colour and space or **depth**, even the way the paint is put onto the canvas, are all investigated, as the history of art, from Edouard Manet to Andy Warhol, is explored in this book.

Impressionism

In the 1860s, young Parisian artists had to have their work accepted by the School of Fine Art and shown at the official Salon exhibitions, if they wanted to become known by the public and make a living. The School of Fine Art was run by a group of men who decided on both the subjects that were painted and the style in which they were painted. This same group would judge the entries for the Salon exhibition, so they had almost complete control over the paintings the public saw.

The French public were accustomed to seeing paintings of flowers, pets, cavalry, inns and portraits, as well as subjects taken from Greek and Roman myths. They were painted in a realistic style, with careful shading in blacks and browns. Accurate and detailed drawing was very important and colours were generally dark. Imaginative painting was discouraged. Landscapes tended to be used only for **backgrounds** and not as subjects themselves.

At the time, Charles Gleyre, a Fine Art teacher, was teaching students such as Auguste Renoir, Claude Monet, Alfred Sisley and Frédéric Bazille at his studio. This group of men, along with Paul Cézanne, Camille Pissarro, Edgar Degas and Edouard Manet were to become known as the Impressionists.

The group's main interest was showing the effects of light and colour on landscapes. Impressionism was an enormous change from the style of painting that the public were used to.

***Le Déjeuner sur l'Herbe*, 1863**
Edouard Manet

This painting, **Lunch on the Grass**, deeply upset the public when it was shown at the 1863 Paris exhibition. Although paintings of the naked female body were exhibited at the time, the figures were generally characters from myths, and the goddess Venus was often shown. What offended people was the subject: a naked woman with clothed men. Also, the people and the clothes were like those seen in Paris in the 1860s rather than mythological.

The unmixed **pure colours** in the painting give a wonderful freshness and feeling of just having been painted. This was one of the first paintings exhibited to show a new style and subject in French art.

Apart from the simple subjects chosen by the artists, their use of colour and paint were also very different. They preferred to use primary colours: red, yellow and blue, and the complementary colours of green, purple and orange. They used short brush strokes of pure unmixed colour, with patches of **contrasting** colour sitting alongside. These colours would blend when seen from a distance, making the paintings appear alive. The paintings gave an impression of the subject, rather than a realistic reproduction.

In 1863, many of the Impressionists entered their paintings for the Salon exhibition. When 3,000 paintings were rejected, there was such an uproar that the French Emperor himself suggested a separate exhibition of these paintings. The reaction from the public and critics was laughter; the display was seen as something to go and poke fun at.

The Impressionists then decided to hold their own exhibition in 1874. Instead of the success they hoped for, they were scorned and insulted by both the public and critics. One of Monet's paintings in the exhibition was called *Impression: Sunrise*, and a critic gave the Impressionists their name from this painting. He thought that it was worse than bad wallpaper! However, the Impressionists continued with their exhibitions and held seven more between 1875 and 1886. By 1886, the public had become used to these paintings with their bright colours and sketchy, unfinished appearance.

Edouard Manet (1832-1883)

Manet became known for producing paintings that upset the public and critics and it was only towards the end of his life that his paintings became popular.

Manet held an exhibition of his work in 1867 and although he supported the Impressionists in their fight for recognition, he did not show his paintings in their exhibitions.

In the late 1860s, Manet became friends with many of the young French Impressionist painters, including Degas, Monet and Cézanne. The group admired

Monet found the perfect subject in his waterlily paintings. The reflecting surface of the water and the rich colour patterns of the lilies has produced a painting of pure colour. The water surface has become flatter and more abstract (looking less like water and more like a pattern).

The landscape does not disappear into the distance as it would in a photograph. Instead, the painting has been tilted up so that the waterlilies seem to float across a flat surface. As a result, the painting can be enjoyed in two ways: as a rich, colourful pattern and as waterlilies floating on water.

Waterlilies (Nymphéas), 1908
Claude Monet

his work and were influenced by it. In turn Manet started to use lighter colours and study the effects of light on his subjects, but always refused to be known as an Impressionist.

In 1890 Manet's painting *Olympia* (1863), was presented to the French by Monet. He felt it was important that such a great work of art should stay in France and said that it was painted by Manet "at the height of his glorious struggle, master of his vision and his craft."

Claude Monet (1840-1926)

Monet preferred studying the effects of light on the landscape rather than painting portraits. He spent his childhood on the French coast, in Le Havre, where he painted seaside scenes and had his pictures displayed in the window of the local picture framer's. These were seen by an artist called Eugène Boudin, who offered Monet help and advice.

In 1862, Monet became friends with Renoir, Sisley and Bazille and they all worked outdoors, painting landscapes.

Over the next few years Monet sold very few paintings. He was always in debt and pleaded with friends to lend him money. He and Pissarro visited London in 1870 where they continued to paint. They were very impressed with the work of the English landscape painters, particularly John Constable and J.M.W. Turner, and the way they, too, showed the effects of light in their paintings. The English reaction to Monet's and Pissarro's work was unenthusiastic, and it was rejected by the Royal Academy in London.

By the 1880s Monet's pictures had started to sell. In 1890 he bought a house at Giverny, not far from Paris, where he planned and created a garden (which is now open to the public) and where he spent the rest of his life.

Monet was fascinated by the effects of light and between 1892 and 1894 he completed 20 paintings of Rouen Cathedral at different times of the day and in different seasons. In one of his paintings of Rouen Cathedral, the shadows have been painted in blues and lilac, rather than dark browns. This

Impressionist method of producing shadows by using different colours, not just darker shades of the same colour, is what gives the paintings their vibrant glow and was to strongly affect future painters.

As his painting developed, Monet concentrated more and more on the quickly-changing effects of light. This meant that the solid shape of his subjects seemed to dissolve and become hazy.

Towards the end of his life Monet had easels built by the lily ponds in his garden, which the gardeners would move around for him as the light changed. Later, these paintings were to be of great interest to **Abstract** painters of the late 1940s and 50s.

Although many other **art movements** appeared and the Impressionists developed their own individual styles, Impressionism itself continued until 1926, when Monet died. His final works, the famous series of waterlily paintings, ended one of the most important periods in the history of art.

ACTIVITY
An Impressionist landscape

• Sketch out a landscape scene, perhaps of trees next to a river or lake. Lightly pencil in the trees, clouds and the line where the trees meet the water.

• Use a small number of watercolours – blue, green, yellow ochre and lilac.

• Let the colours run into each other to create a hazy effect of light.

• When the mingled colours are dry, apply stronger coloured dark areas and reflections.

9

Post-Impressionism

During the Impressionist period there were many artists who created their own individual style of painting and so could not be called Impressionists. They knew about the Impressionists and their use of bright colours, but they did not want to concentrate on painting the effects of light alone. Three of these artists, Cézanne, Paul Gauguin and Vincent van Gogh painted pictures which still influence the styles of the 20th century.

Paul Cézanne (1839-1906)

Cézanne lived in Aix-en-Provence, a town 650 kilometres from Paris. His work could only be seen in Paris in a small, dark room at the back of an art materials shop. Cézanne had enough money to support himself and did not have to sell his paintings to make a living, unlike other artists of the time.

Cézanne started to work with Pissarro in 1872 and his paintings began to show the influence of the Impressionists. Although he studied the effects of light, Cézanne was much more interested in the solid look of his subjects. He wanted them to keep their shape, rather than dissolving in a haze of colour like the Impressionist paintings. The arrangement of shapes was important to Cézanne and he would often change things for the sake of his painting. He would tilt books and bottles, and make doors and tables such odd shapes that a carpenter would find it difficult to make them.

The Blue Vase, 1885-87
Paul Cézanne

By the time Cézanne painted **The Blue Vase**, he had developed his own distinctive style. In this painting, the colour has been put on by using very small, careful brush strokes. They have not been smudged or blended but sit side by side. Cézanne has made the objects look solid by shading with little patches of colour. For example, the walls and table are made up of very delicate colour changes.

The painting has been very carefully arranged and to move any one of these shapes would upset the balance of the picture. Cézanne needed a darker shape on the left to balance the darkness of the flowers in the middle and the darker bands on the right. To use a whole bottle would be too much so he painted the bottle as thought it were cut in half.

The blue in the vase has also been used in the background and in the shadows on the table. The flower stem on the top right (which is similar to the shape of the vase) connects the flowers to the panel on the right.

Although Cézanne tried to show the shapes of his subjects as clearly as possible, towards the end of his life, his painting become **flatter**. In these later paintings there is no longer a subject on a background. In the watercolour of *Mont Sainte-Victoire* (1900) the sky and mountain have been painted in little patches of colour to show their shape. The late paintings of Cézanne had a strong effect on the early Cubist painters.

In 1895 Cézanne was persuaded to have a large exhibition at a gallery belonging to Ambroise Vollard. It was his first exhibition since 1877 and was much admired by the older Impressionists – Monet, Renoir, Degas and Pissarro – and also by younger artists, including Henri Matisse.

Paul Gauguin (1848-1903)

Gauguin did not start painting seriously until he was 34 years old. The influence of Cézanne and of Japanese prints can be seen in his early paintings. Japanese prints, or coloured woodcuts, were very popular in France during the late 19th century. The **flat colours**, curling lines and the rich patterns and textures found in these prints were admired by many artists.

In his paintings, Gauguin used strong outlines, little shading and bright primary colours. He said to one of his friends, "Do not paint too closely from nature." In other words, the artist must not simply copy something they have seen; they must paint their own world, as they see it through the imagination.

Later on in his life, Gauguin lived in Tahiti in the South Pacific. Here the clear bright colours and the bold patterns and shapes of the tropical landscape became an ideal subject.

Gauguin said of his painting, "I want to try anything." This wish to experiment and use the imagination was also to become very important to later 20th century painters.

Women of Tahiti (On the Beach), 1891
Paul Gauguin

This painting shows Gauguin's fascination with the Tahitian people and their surroundings.

As with all his work, the paint has been applied quite thinly but there is a very strong feeling of pattern and shape. The figures in the foreground are clear and have been painted with bright colours. The red and white skirt and the lilac dress contrast strongly with the yellow of the beach and the greens of the sea.

*As with Japanese prints, the whole **composition** has been kept flat.*

Vincent van Gogh (1853-1890)

Copies of van Gogh's paintings are as popular today as those of the Impressionists. Yet, during his short lifetime, he sold only one painting.

Throughout his life he felt a very strong bond with peasants and farm workers and his paintings often recorded the way they lived. His first pictures were dark and serious, but in 1886 he went to Paris to live with his brother, Theo, who was an art dealer. There he was influenced by the work of the Impressionists and also by Gauguin.

In 1888, attracted by the sun, he went to live in Arles in the South of France. Here he worked almost nonstop, his brush strokes becoming broader and his colours brighter. He started to use strong yellows, blues and greens. Sometimes he would even set up his easel in the fields at night so he could continue painting the landscape and recording the effects of the night.

He was joined by Gauguin in Arles, but after a few months they started to have violent arguments. On one occassion, van Gogh threatened Gauguin with a razor and felt so sorry for what he had done that he cut off part of his own ear. He suffered from spells of madness and soon after finishing *Crows in the Wheatfields* (1890), he shot himself and died two days later.

In his paintings van Gogh showed moods and emotions through colour. His **still lifes**, landscapes and portraits have been painted with brilliant colour and deep feeling for the subject. A great gift of van Gogh's was his ability to take a simple object, such as a chair, and produce an unforgettable **image**.

Up to the 19th century, mood or feeling in painting was generally shown by dramatic action or the expression on people's faces. Van Gogh created expression and feeling through his use of colour, expressive brushwork and **textured** paint, and he influenced many later artists in the 20th century.

Pointillism

Impressionism had an effect on many artists who went on to develop a wide variety of styles. Georges Seurat, Paul Signac and Henri Edmond Cross developed a style known as Pointillism.

These paintings do not use brush strokes but are made up of tiny dots of pure colour on a white background. The viewer's eye blends the dots to make solid shapes. Printed pictures in books and newspapers use the same **technique** – the individual dots can be seen through a microscope or magnifying glass.

Seurat concentrated on paintings of holiday scenes, which were a traditional subject of the Impressionists.

ACTIVITY
An interior

● Plan an arrangement so that one object is not right in the middle of the paper.

● Keep the shapes flat with just enough shading to show the shapes of the objects.

● Use bright colours with strong patterns.

Fauvism

The name Fauves, or 'Wild Beasts', was given to a group of artists by a critic who saw one of their exhibitions in Paris in 1905. Amongst the exhibits was a sculpture rather like one done by a much earlier sculptor called Donatello. The critic came into the room and exclaimed, "Well, Donatello and the wild beasts." The critic was not finding fault with the artists' style but the name stuck. The person who bought Matisse's *Woman in a Hat (Madame Matisse)* (1905), which was in the exhibition, described it as, "a thing brilliant and powerful, but the nastiest smear of paint I have ever seen."

The Fauves used violent contrasts of brilliant colour. Shapes were shown by using colour and line rather than by using light and dark. Whereas the Impressionists would use delicate changes of colour to show light and shade, the Fauves put red next to green and brilliant yellows next to purples.

Trees could be red, yellow or blue, skies could be orange, and portraits could contain a whole variety of colours. The colours were painted without any blending or softening.

Maurice de Vlaminck (1876-1958)

One of the artists whose work was in the Paris exhibition of 1905 was Maurice de Vlaminck. Before becoming an artist, he had taught himself to paint and had earned a living from playing the violin.

A Barge on the River Seine, 1906
Maurice de Vlaminck

Vlaminck has used thick brush strokes of contrasting colour to produce a painting which is very wild and free. Successful paintings like this have a strong effect on the viewer, who can imagine the movement of the water and the smoke from the chimney.

There is a great difference between this painting and a French landscape of 60 years earlier. Instead of the landscape being seen in a realistic way, with lights, darks, shadows and deep space, it is a pattern of violent contrasting colour.

The colour contrasts – the red and blue of the barge, the blue and white of the water and the strong, distinct brush strokes – are as important as the actual subject.

Vlaminck was a great admirer of van Gogh's work. He had seen an exhibition of his work in 1901 and thought of van Gogh as the father of Fauvism. He felt that he painted with great freedom. Vlaminck declared he would do the same and, "paint with his heart and guts without worrying about style."

Henri Matisse (1869-1954)

Another artist in the 1905 exhibition was Henri Matisse. He had seen the Cézanne exhibition in 1895 and also studied the work of Gauguin and van Gogh. In 1903 he saw some of the Pointillist paintings of Signac and Cross and he started to use a similar technique using broader brushstrokes. Although Matisse painted with the same bright colours as Vlaminck, his work was much more careful and controlled.

In 1905 he went to the South of France and produced some very unusual paintings. In the portrait of his wife, *Green Stripe (Madame Matisse)* (1905), instead of using light and shade to show the shape and form of the head, he has used colour. Rather than using dark shading down the front of the face, he has used a green stripe. The use of colour in this painting has been very carefully thought out.

When writing about his painting, Matisse said, "What I strive for is expression, not the expression of a human face or violent movement. It is the whole arrangement of my picture, the position of the figures, the space, they all play their part."

In 1931 Matisse was asked to produce a very large **mural** called *The Dance*. When it was finished it was found that he had worked to the wrong measurements. Matisse produced a second version, but to help him arrange the picture, he painted areas of flat colour on pieces of paper which he could move around and reposition. When he was satisfied with the composition, he could then begin the final painting.

Many years later, in 1947, he started using coloured paper again. Matisse described it as, "drawing with scissors" and said that it reminded him of a sculptor's work. These paper cut-outs, which are sometimes just one colour against a plain background, often have a feeling of dance-like movement which comes from the relationship between the colours. Matisse said, "I have worked all my life, in order that people might say, 'It seems so simple to do'."

Unlike many artists, by the time he died, Matisse was popular around the world. His work was admired by art collectors, critics and younger artists of the time.

ACTIVITY
A Fauve still life

• Paint brightly coloured flowers as broadly and freely as you can, using your imagination or the real thing.

• Allow the bright colours to reach every part of the picture: the flowers, container and background.

• Try and use maximum colour contrasts such as orange with green, red with blue, blue with orange.

Cubism

Cézanne's final works were rather like **mosaics** of strong patches of colour. Although the subjects in his paintings can be clearly seen, they are broken up into small shapes. Cézanne's late works were studied by two artists: Georges Braque and Pablo Picasso, who were to develop the style known as Cubism.

At an exhibition of Braque's painting in Paris in 1908, one critic described him as, "reducing everything to geometrical diagrams, to cubes."

Cubist paintings do not try to show detail or exact copies of objects; the artists created their own imaginary worlds using geometrical shapes like cubes and cones. Until 1914, when some artists started to use brighter colours, they used greys, browns, greens and yellows and sometimes just painted in black and white.

Georges Braque (1882-1963)

Braque was initially influenced by the Fauvists, particularly Matisse. In 1908 his attention moved to Cézanne and for the next five years he concentrated on the effects of light. Braque and Picasso worked together from 1909 until 1914. They produced similar work using neutral colours and complicated patterns of geometrical shapes.

In Braque's *Still Life with Violin and Pitcher* (1910), the subject is broken up and shown as an arrangement of smaller overlapping shapes. Instead of having **foreground** and background, the whole

Houses at L'Estaque, 1908
Georges Braque

This picture looks rather like a late painting by Cézanne. Every object in the landscape appears solid and very geometrical in shape.

Rather than being painted in detail, the tree trunk, leaves and houses have become flattened shapes, all locking into one another.

There is very little space between the foreground and the background, and all the lights and darks are the same strength or tone.

In this painting the subjects have been taken apart, looked at from different angles and put back together in a completely new way, although the various pieces of the violin and guitar can still be seen.

Picasso has made the subjects partly disappear. He has created an imaginary world where pattern and shape, lights and darks, textures, colour and the arrangement, or composition, are cleverly combined.

Violin and Guitar, 1913
Pablo Picasso

surface of the painting is flattened and has a strong pattern of lights and darks.

Braque and Picasso went on to create 'papiers colles' or collage. They made pictures from everyday materials such as newspapers, labels and pieces of cloth, stuck to a board or canvas.

Pablo Picasso (1881-1973)

Picasso became one of the greatest artists of the 20th century. He often visited Paris and became interested in the street life. His paintings of people in cafés and dance halls were often painted in different shades of blue. The years 1900-1902 became known as his Blue Period.

In 1904 he moved to Paris and changed to using shades of red and pink. Many of his subjects were of characters from the circus, which he often visited.

Picasso produced more than 20,000 works. He rebelled against traditional painting – although he used the same subject matter: still lifes, nudes, landscapes and animals, he painted them in very unusual ways.

ACTIVITY
A Cubist stereo

● Draw an everyday object, for example, a personal stereo, but 'reinvent' it in the Cubist style.

● Take various pieces from the stereo and headphones and put them back together in a different order.

● Words can also be used.

● Use two colours, such as black and yellow. The third colour is the white of the paper.

Expressionism

The Expressionists were a group of artists who painted in very different styles, but they all changed or distorted shapes to create strange and disturbing worlds. They used brilliant colour like the Fauvists and flattened space like the Cubists.

Edvard Munch (1863-1944)

Edvard Munch was born in Norway but studied for a short time in Paris where he admired the work of van Gogh, Gauguin and Seurat. Munch was an anxious man who tended to worry about life, especially about feelings of loneliness.

Many of his paintings show images of illness and death. His first exhibition in Germany, in 1892, was closed by the authorities because they were so shocked by his work. Munch returned to Norway in 1909 where his work became calmer and more relaxed.

James Ensor (1860-1949)

The Belgian painter, James Ensor, was producing strange Expressionist paintings as early as 1888. He did not seem to like his fellow men, so he showed them as masks and skeletons dressed in rags, doing very odd things, as the titles *Skeletons Trying to Get Warm* and *Skeletons Quarrelling over a Herring* suggest. Ensor used loud, garish colours and broken brush strokes which made his work seem quite violent.

In this painting there is a strong feeling of people being alone in an unhappy world. This has been produced by using curving, sad lines and 'unreal' colour.

Like van Gogh, Munch used colour to express the feelings of human beings. Instead of being happy and positive, the bright colours used in the girls' dresses seem to separate the figures from the rest of the world. This sad and lonely feeling can be seen in much of Munch's early work.

Girls on a Bridge, 1905
Edvard Munch

25

The Bridge Group

In Germany, in 1905, a group of young artists called Die Brücke (the Bridge) was formed which developed Expressionist ideas even further. Most of the group were not trained in art, but they showed their strong feelings and lively imaginations through harsh colour and distorted shapes. They were influenced by the late Impressionists, African and Pacific art and the colours they used showed the **influence** of the Fauves, particularly Vlaminck.

Some of the most powerful images the German Expressionists produced were black and white woodcuts. The wood was gouged out or cut away to make an image which was then covered in ink and printed onto paper. Emil Nolde's *The Steam Trawler* (1910), is a good example of how a feeling for the water, sky and boat can be strongly expressed by a simple method.

Ernst Kirchner (1880-1938)

Kirchner was one of the leading artists of the Bridge group. He painted both portraits and landscapes. His work has a restless feel to it which is produced by his use of jagged shapes and strong colours. The figures in his paintings can often seem rather sad and thoughtful, as if they are thinking about an unhappy future.

In Kirchner's painting *Self-portrait with Model* (1907), the strong, clashing colours have been almost flung down on the canvas, without trying to soften or blend them. Although the hard-edged shapes are painted in brilliant colour, they are quite similar to the jagged shape of black and white woodcuts.

During the Second World War, the German Nazis disapproved of Kirchner's work and confiscated 600 of his paintings. Soon after, Kirchner committed suicide.

*This is thought to be one of Kirchner's finest paintings although it does not have traditional shading, **perspective** or a neat finish.*

In some areas the canvas has hardly been covered; shapes have been left roughly finished and the paint sometimes goes over the edges. But it is because these areas of colour, shape and line are so carefully planned, that the overall effect is of a powerful painting,

Marcella, **1909-10**
Ernst Kirchner

The Blue Rider Group

Other artists whose work is generally included in German Expressionism are the group known as Der Blaue Reiter (The Blue Rider), which was formed in Munich in 1911. These artists included Alexi Jawlensky, Wassily Kandinsky, Franz Marc, Auguste Macke and Paul Klee. The group got its name from Kandinsky's love of blue and Marc's love of horses. Jawlensky and Kandinsky had both lived in Paris and were deeply impressed by Matisse.

Wassily Kandinsky (1866-1944)

Kandinsky was born in Russia but studied art in Munich, Germany. During a trip to Paris in 1909, he saw the work of the Post-Impressionists and the Fauves. His early paintings show the influence of these two movements. In these paintings of gardens and landscapes, the image of the landscape can be clearly seen, but the shapes, lines and colours he uses are also very important. Some of the paintings are halfway between Abstract paintings and paintings of an actual subject. Kandinsky did not seem sure whether to paint a subject or simply to drop it altogether.

Around 1913 he started to produce paintings that were the first completely Abstract works in modern art. He often got his inspiration from listening to music and the paintings did not contain images of any objects at all.

After the First World War, Kandinsky's Abstract works became more Geometric. He used sharp outlines and clear patterns. *Composition VIII No. 260* (1923) is composed just of lines, circles and arcs.

Kandinsky influenced other artists through his paintings and also through his work as an art teacher.

Paul Klee (1879-1940)

Klee was one of the most original masters of modern art. His early works were black and white etchings and pencil sketches of landscapes, which showed the influence of the Impressionists. After a trip to North Africa in 1914, Klee started to use more colour and produced paintings of very delicate, harmonious colours.

Many of his ideas grew out of the paintings as he worked on them. He described one method that he used as "taking a line for a walk." His work *Twittering Machine* (1922), is an example of this technique, with its connecting lines and circular shapes.

Although he was influenced by the work of his fellow artists, his own work is easy to recognise. It often has a dreamlike, fantasy feel to it and has been composed and painted with great thought and care. Sometimes he gave his paintings amusing titles such as *A Guardian Angel Serves a Modest Breakfast* (1920).

ACTIVITY
An Expressionist portrait

• Try to draw a self portrait in front of a mirror.

• Use a limited colour range – this example has used yellow ochre, black, green, pink and white.

• Don't worry about keeping to the edges or going over them. This is all about being bold and direct.

Surrealism

Dadaism

In 1916 a group of artists and writers gathered together in Zürich, Switzerland and formed the movement known as Dadaism. The word *dada* means hobby horse in French and is said to have been chosen at random from a dictionary.
It became an international movement with groups in Paris, Berlin, New York and Hanover.

Dadaism developed in different ways in the various cities but its main aim was to protest against tradition. The Dadaists were against the idea of fine art and of famous paintings only being seen in museums and galleries. What the artists did, through music, literature and theatre, could be described as a kind of deliberate nonsense and was often done to shock their audiences.

The Dadaists felt that everyday objects were works of art. In 1913, the French artist Marcel Duchamp exhibited his first 'ready made' sculpture: a bicycle wheel. The Dadaists did not feel that painting alone was a revolutionary enough way of expressing their ideas. The painted images they did produce often showed strange machines which had no practical use at all. One was Francis Picabia's ridiculous but very accurate gadget called *A Compressed Air Brake or Machine for Cracking Peach Stones* (1917). This was a way of poking fun at technology and the whole idea of producing machines.

Collage was very popular with the

Dadaists. The German artist Kurt Schwitters produced very powerful works in this **medium** by using materials like paper, string, wood, metal, feathers, financial documents and bus tickets.

Despite the Dadaists' dislike of museums and fine art, much of their work ended up where they did not want it to be – in a fine art museum.

Surrealism

Dadaism was replaced by a new movement in Paris in 1922 called Surrealism. The French poet Guillaume Apollinaire first used the word 'surrealist' meaning 'beyond the real'. The early Surrealist movement was formed by a group of writers and poets, together with painters and sculptors. Like the Dadaists, they set out to explore the hidden depths of the mind. However, unlike Dadaism, Surrealism was not against traditional art.

Surrealist painters created dream-like images showing strange and impossible situations. Some of these works have a nightmarish feeling about them. Sometimes the artists used very **realistic** detail but the various parts were combined in an unrealistic way. With Surrealism, paintings have subjects, but they have been painted in strange, unreal ways.

Although Paris was the centre of Surrealism, the most important artists were Max Ernst (German), René Magritte (Belgian), Joan Miró and Salvador Dalí (Spanish).

Max Ernst (1891-1976)

Ernst produced paintings with monstrous creatures, strange forests and bleak cities, all drawn from deep within his imagination. Some of these images are taken from the world described by science fiction writers.

During his career as an artist, Ernst experimented with many different media. In all his works he tried to show the fantastic world of dreams and the imagination.

René Magritte (1898-1967)

Magritte's painting, like Dalí's, also show familiar things in odd places: this style of painting became known as 'magic realism' and Magritte was the main artist to use the technique. The effect is strange and confusing. In one of his paintings *Time Transfixed* (1939), a steam engine comes out of a fireplace. In another, *Son of Man* (1964), the head and shoulders of a man are shown against a cloudy sky, but the face is partly hidden by a freshly picked apple.

Magritte made fun of famous works of art by painting Surrealist versions. In *Madame Récamier de David* (1949), he replaced the reclining woman in the original portrait, by Jacques Louis David, with a coffin.

His technique is more realistic, using lights, darks and fine detail, but his subjects are not at all traditional.

Salvador Dalí (1904-1989)

Dalí worked in a Surrealist style from 1929. His paintings often show everyday objects in unusual forms, for example the extraordinary images of limp watches, eerie landscapes and blazing giraffes. His works contain realistic detail and are very colourful.

Dalí moved to New York from Spain in 1940 and spent the next eight years in the United States. His later paintings often had religious themes.

Other artists in the Surrealist movement criticised Dalí for being too concerned with selling his paintings and making money.

Dalí also produced Surrealist films, illustrated and wrote books, made jewellery and designed theatrical costumes and sets.

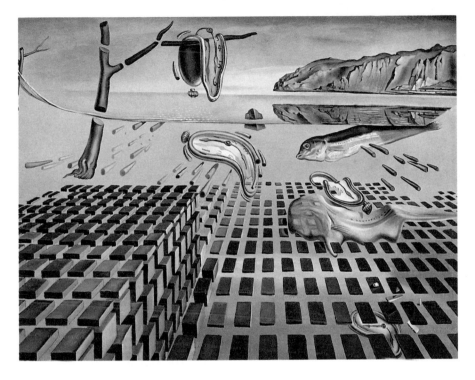

This painting, with its strange landscape and odd combination of objects, is rather like a photograph of a dream. It shows real things in a totally unexpected and disturbing way. Something that the viewer is likely to see and use in everyday life has been totally changed and put in an extraordinary setting.

The Disintegration of the Persistence of Memory, 1952-54
Salvador Dalí

Harlequin's Carnival, 1924-25
Joan Miró

In this painting, a whole range of strange creatures are shown in a simple and flatly painted room. These creatures include a snake, a bird's head, a white hand, a ladder, some cats playing with string, a fish and an ear.

Instead of using a realistic light and shade technique, Miró's creatures are flat and are shown in a very shallow background.

The coloured areas have been chosen with great care. The blacks, blues, reds, yellows and whites all swirl about creating a 'dance' of their own. The combination of this colourful pattern with the very original subjects has produced an extraordinary painting.

Joan Miró (1893-1983)

Miró was the artist who did the most to mix Surrealist ideas with other styles in early 20th century painting. In his work before 1920, he included the bright colours of the Fauves and the shapes of Cubism. He was also influenced by art he had seen in Spanish churches.

After moving to Paris in 1920, he mixed with Surrealist writers and developed his style further.

In a technological age, Miró's paintings have a very untechnological feel to them. His stars, suns and moons and small people are similar to cave drawings and children's art. The images he produced in the period just before the Second World War, have a dark, threatening side to them.

Miró used a limited number of bright colours, especially red, blue, green, yellow and black on neutral coloured backgrounds. He worked in many media including watercolour, pastel and collage.

ACTIVITY
A Surrealist apple

● Think of some everyday objects. Imagine these objects in an unusual or unlikely situation and then draw them. In this example, an apple, which is usually eaten, is eating some chips!

● Draw carefully so that your idea can be understood. Keep the colours flat.

● A pen and coloured inks have been used in this example.

Abstract Art

The forms of Abstract painting varied enormously. Some painters were influenced by Kandinsky and his colourful composition, others by the very opposite – Mondrian and Geometric Abstraction.

Geometric Abstraction

After the Second World War, new developments in art took place in the United States. This happened for two main reasons. Firstly, many well-known European artists went to live or stay in the United States after the war. Secondly, the United States Government provided money to support and encourage the arts.

In New York, in 1945, the two most important styles of painting were Geometric Abstraction and Surrealism. European artists, working in both these styles, came to New York. Amongst the Abstract painters, Mondrian's arrival was greeted with great enthusiasm and his works were widely admired by other artists and the public. His arrival encouraged new interest in Geometric Abstraction which had been popular in the United States in the 1930s.

The arrival of the Surrealists made an even bigger impression. The painter Roberto Matta went to the United States in 1939, followed in the early 1940s by Ernst, André Masson and Dalí. In 1942, Ernst's wife, Peggy Guggenheim, set up a gallery and museum in New York, called *Art of this Century*. The opening exhibition included works by many of the most important Surrealist and Abstract artists of the 20th century.

Piet Mondrian (1872-1944)

The Dutch painter, Mondrian, was briefly influenced by the Cubism of Braque and Picasso. However, unlike them, he did not want to produce images of real objects. His painting called *Composition* (1921), was made up of a grid of black lines together with flat areas of grey and primary colours. Mondrian continued with this style of painting almost until the end of his life.

In spite of Mondrian's inventiveness, much of the art produced after the war in Paris by other artists was quite traditional. Many painters produced works which they knew would be accepted by the public, rather than experimenting and trying new things.

Abstract Expressionism

From 1942 to 1947, the New York gallery, *Art of this Century*, showed the work of young American artists alongside that of the Europeans. These artists, who included Jackson Pollock, Robert Motherwell, Mark Rothko, Clyfford Still and Adolph Gottlieb had a major influence on the development of new painting. The artists were based in New York and the Abstract Expressionist movement was also known as the New York school.

The artists were influenced by the work of Kandinsky and the Surrealists. Although their styles were quite varied, there were two main types of Abstract Expressionism. The 'action painters' concentrated on the texture of the paint and the movements of their hands as they worked. Some painters, like Pollock, used drips and spatters of paint. Others, like Willem de Kooning and Franz Josef Kline, used broad brush strokes of thick paint.

The American 'colour field painters' concentrated on colour and shape. Artists like Rothko, Barnett Newman and Still used huge 'fields' of colour. Rothko's paintings are made up of rectangles of colour which seem to glow, as though they have an invisible light source. The splendour and richness of these paintings is amazing as they seem so simple.

Abstract Expressionism also developed in Europe with two main groups of artists. Tachism concentrated on patches of colour and got its name from 'tache', the French word for spot. 'Art informel' – French for informal art – was similar to the action painting of New York.

By 1960, Abstract Expressionism had been accepted as a new style of painting. Although the development of large 'colour field' paintings continued with painters like Helen Frankenthaler, Morris Louis and Kenneth Noland, other approaches began to appear.

At the end of the Second World War, Paris remained the artistic capital of the world. Abstract art was the most important style; painting an actual subject became less popular, as did Surrealism. However, one part of Surrealism that was still important
was automatic drawing. This was the idea of working without trying to control what happens.

Jackson Pollock (1912-1956)

Pollock's early work was strongly influenced by Picasso and some of the Surrealists. He spent time travelling around the country and produced realistic paintings of American scenes. He was very interested in the images produced by Native Americans – particularly the sand-paintings of the Navajo people.

Pollock was one of the first artists to work with the canvas spread out flat on the ground. After 1947, he did not paint directly onto the canvas but dripped paint from a container with holes in the bottom or from a trowel or stick.

The new and very different method of dripping paint completely changed the appearance of painting. The painting is a web of lines, blobs and splashes, all swirling about in dance-like rhythms.

There is no subject on a background. The feelings of the artist are shown by the rhythms and layers of paint on the surface.

Untitled no. 2, 1942-1944
Jackson Pollock

Robert Rauschenberg (born 1925) and Jasper Johns (born 1930)

These two American artists played an important part in the move from Abstract Expressionism to Pop Art. They started to show images from everyday life in their work.

Rauschenberg said that he wanted to "fill the gap between art and life." His collage paintings contain photographs, fabrics and torn newspaper. Some paintings have an actual object, such as a chain or a bird attached to them.

Johns' first exhibition in 1958 contained images of flags and targets, all painted in quite a detailed way. Like Rauschenberg, Johns used real objects, such as rulers and compasses, attached to his paintings.

ACTIVITY
An Abstract painting

• Use primary colour poster paints and also black and white.

• Paint a background by allowing the red and yellow paints to run together while still wet.

• Allow this to dry.

• Paint the blue, black and white shapes over the top of the background.

• Smaller spots of pure colour can be flicked on with the brush.

Pop Art

The British artist, Richard Hamilton, was very interested in the work of the Dadaist, Duchamp. The subjects of his pictures came from the images produced by the mass media: newspapers and television, and products that were part of everyday life.

The work produced by Hamilton, Rauschenberg and Johns influenced a group of artists, working in both London and New York, who came to be known as Pop (short for popular) Artists.

The British Pop Artists, Peter Blake, David Hockney, Allen Jones and Patrick Caulfield, used images from modern life. Hockney produced *Typhoo Tea* (1960), one of the earliest paintings to show a commercial product with a brand name. Blake painted rock stars and designed record sleeves. These images showed the lifestyles of the time and were very popular.

In the United States, the American Pop Art style was developed by artists like Roy Lichtenstein, Claes Oldenburg, James Rosenquist and Andy Warhol.

With the Pop Artists, everyday life was brought into art. They painted what they saw around them and took their images from advertisements, billboards, comic books, movies and television. Because these images were so familiar to the public, Pop Art in the United States was a great success.

Campbell's Soup Can 19, 1962
Andy Warhol

This is one of a number of almost identical paintings done by the artist in the early 1960s. The style is quite cartoon-like and the image is very flat and simple.

Warhol's images of Campbell's soup cans, Coca-Cola bottles and cardboard boxes show his experiences of the advertising world, where he once worked. He also did silk-screen prints of popular entertainers such as Elvis Presley and Marilyn Monroe.

Roy Lichtenstein (born 1923)

Lichtenstein's early work was in the Abstract Expressionist style. After 1957, he started to use enlarged images of instructions, which makes the viewer reconsider everyday subjects as works of art. He also used characters from original comic strips like *Whaam!* (1963). These were painted in dots of bright primary colours, copying printing techniques.

Andy Warhol (1928-1987)

Warhol was a film maker as well as a painter and was the most influential of the Pop Artists. His images are very similar in style to Duchamp's Dadaist works.

Warhol felt that the objects and products of everyday life were art. These popular images do not have to be changed but should be seen as they are – like Duchamp's bicycle wheel. It is not so much *what* we are looking at, but the *way* we look at it. Is it an everyday object or is it a work of art?

Open the door by pushing the door button.

ACTIVITY
A Pop Art instruction guide

- Draw a step-by-step guide of how to work a washing machine.

- Draw out the image in pencil in a clean cartoon style.

- Include written instructions.

- Do the final drawing in a fine ink or felt tip line, using a ruler for the straight edges.

- Use felt tip or poster paints to show simple areas of bright flat colour.

Conclusion

The history of 20th century painting has attracted a lot of labels. It seems that people have to give something a name to be able to understand it. However, it does not really matter whether a painting belongs to a particular art movement; what does matter is whether it is a product of real feeling and has the power to affect the viewer.

New art and images are sometimes puzzling and need to be thought about carefully. Understanding painting is like reading or writing – it has to be learned.

From a very young age, the art of painting or making marks, seems to be an important part of human activity.

A writer talking about some magnificent late Ice-Age paintings of animals, said that it looked as though the act of painting was more important than the result. Standing in front of a huge drip painting by Jackson Pollock, it would seem that very little has changed over the last 20,000 years.

GLOSSARY

Abstract
a painting with shapes and lines rather than people or objects

Art Movement
a group of artists, who share the same aims and beliefs

Background
the area behind the main object(s)

Collage
a picture made by sticking pieces of cloth, paper, etc., onto a surface

Composition
the arrangement of shapes, lines and colours in a painting

Contrasting
colours which are very different from each other

Depth
the amount of space that can be seen in a painting

Flat
an object in a painting that does not appear three-dimensional

Flat colour
colour that does not vary in shade or tone

Foreground
the area in a painting closest to the viewer

Influence
the effect of other artists on art movements

Image
a painting or drawing of something or someone

Medium (plural: media)
the materials used to create a picture

Mosaic
a design or picture made by putting small coloured pieces onto a surface

Mural
a painting done on a wall, rather than on a canvas or paper

Perspective
making things look smaller in the distance and larger in the foreground

Pure colour
a colour that is not mixed with another

Realistic
showing objects in a true-to-life way

Still life
painting of objects that cannot move, for example, flowers, fruit, bowls, musical instruments, etc.

Technique
the way in which paint is applied

Textured
a rough surface made by using thick paint

INDEX

INDEX OF PAINTINGS